BACKYARD CHICKEN KEEPING FOR BEGINNERS

A Comprehensive Guide To Planning, Raising Healthy Hens, And Caring For Your Flock & Maximizing Egg Production

Ethan Harry

Table of Contents

CHAPTER ONE

INTRODUCTION TO BACKYARD CHICKEN KEEPING

Backyard chicken keeping is becoming increasingly popular as more people discover the joys and benefits of raising their own chickens. It's a rewarding hobby that provides fresh eggs, helps with pest control, and offers an opportunity to learn about animal husbandry. Whether you're looking for a sustainable way to source your own eggs or simply want to experience the pleasure of keeping chickens, this guide will introduce you to the basics of backyard chicken keeping.

First and foremost, it's important to understand that chickens require care and attention, just like any other pet.

They need a safe and comfortable environment to thrive. A well-built coop is essential to protect them from predators and harsh weather. Inside the coop, chickens need nesting boxes for laying eggs and roosting bars for sleeping. Adequate space is crucial; a cramped environment can lead to stress and health issues among the flock.

Feeding your chickens a balanced diet is key to their health and egg production. Chickens primarily eat grains, but they also enjoy kitchen scraps and greens, which can supplement their diet. Fresh water should always be available to keep them hydrated.

Chickens are social animals, so it's best to keep at least three to six hens. This allows them to establish a natural pecking order and provides company for one another. Regular interaction with your chickens helps them stay tame and friendly, making them a delightful addition to your backyard.

Keeping chickens also involves regular maintenance, such as cleaning the coop, collecting eggs, and monitoring their health. Common health issues include mites, lice, and respiratory problems, but with proper care and attention, these can be managed effectively.

Backyard chicken keeping can be a fulfilling and educational experience. It connects you with nature and offers a simple way to practice sustainable living. Whether you have a spacious garden or a small urban yard, with the right preparation and care, you can enjoy the many benefits of having your own flock of chickens.

HISTORY AND BENEFITS OF KEEPING CHICKENS

The practice of keeping chickens has a long and storied history, tracing back thousands of years when humans first domesticated these birds primarily for their eggs and meat. Chickens became a staple of rural life, providing a reliable source of nutrition. This tradition has persisted through the ages, with chickens continuing to play a crucial role in agriculture and daily life across various cultures and regions.

In recent years, there has been a notable resurgence in the popularity of backyard chicken keeping. This renewed interest is largely driven by a growing desire for organic and locally-sourced food, sustainable living practices, and a deeper connection to where our food comes from. As more people become concerned with the quality and origins of their food, the appeal of raising chickens at home has grown significantly.

The benefits of keeping chickens are manifold and extend beyond simply having a supply of fresh eggs. One of the primary advantages is the superior quality of the eggs produced by backyard chickens. These eggs are often fresher, more nutritious, and tastier compared to those found in stores. Home-raised eggs typically have richer yolks and higher levels of beneficial nutrients, as the chickens' diet can be controlled and varied to include healthy scraps and grains.

In addition to providing eggs, chickens contribute to natural pest control. They have a voracious appetite for insects and weeds, helping to keep these nuisances in check within your yard or garden. This can significantly reduce the need for chemical pesticides, promoting a healthier and more eco-friendly environment.

Another significant benefit of raising chickens is the production of rich manure. Chicken manure is an excellent source of nutrients for gardening and can be composted to create high-quality fertilizer. This not only helps to improve soil fertility but also supports a sustainable cycle of food production and waste management within a household.

Moreover, keeping chickens can be an incredibly rewarding and educational experience for families. It provides a unique opportunity for children to learn about responsibility, animal care, and the natural world. Interacting with chickens and observing their behaviors can teach valuable lessons about biology and ecology, fostering a greater appreciation for nature.

LEGAL CONSIDERATIONS AND REGULATIONS

Starting a backyard chicken flock involves more than just setting up a coop and purchasing birds; it requires a thorough understanding of the legal considerations and regulations specific to your locality. Chicken keeping laws can vary significantly from one place to another, so it is essential to be well-informed about the rules governing this practice in your area to avoid any legal complications.

One of the first steps in ensuring compliance is to research your local laws and ordinances. Many cities and counties have specific regulations that dictate how many chickens you can keep, the type of housing they require, and whether or not you can keep roosters. Roosters, in particular, are often subject to restrictions due to noise concerns, which can lead to complaints from neighbors. In some areas, roosters are entirely prohibited within city limits. Checking with your city or county government is a crucial part of this process. This can often be done by visiting the city hall, contacting the local zoning office, or searching your local government's website. These resources can provide detailed information on the rules that apply to backyard chicken keeping in your area. Some municipalities may require you to obtain a permit to keep chickens, while others may have regulations based on the size of your property or the proximity of your chicken coop to your neighbors' homes. For instance, there may be minimum space requirements for each bird, stipulations about how far the coop must be from property lines, or restrictions on the total number of chickens allowed per household. These regulations are in place to ensure that the chickens are kept in humane conditions and to minimize any potential nuisances or health risks to the community.

Understanding and adhering to these regulations is essential not only to avoid fines or penalties but also to foster good relationships with your neighbors and the local community. Keeping informed about any changes in local laws is also important, as ordinances can be updated or modified over time. Engaging with local chicken-keeping groups or online forums can be a valuable way to stay informed and share experiences with other chicken keepers in your area.

CHOOSING THE RIGHT BREED FOR YOUR NEEDS

Selecting the right breed of chicken is crucial to ensuring your specific needs and expectations are met. With hundreds of chicken breeds available, each with its own unique traits, it's important to choose a breed that aligns with your goals, whether they are for egg production, meat, dual-purpose, hardiness in different climates, or even ornamental value.

For those primarily interested in egg production, certain breeds stand out for their prolific laying abilities. The Rhode Island Red, Leghorn, and Australorp are particularly renowned for their egg-laying prowess. Rhode Island Reds are hardy, adaptable, and produce a substantial number of brown eggs. Leghorns, especially the white variety, are famous for their high egg production, often laying large quantities of white eggs. Australorps are also excellent layers, known for their calm demeanor and consistent production of brown eggs.

If your goal is meat production, breeds like the Cornish Cross or Plymouth Rock are excellent choices. Cornish Cross chickens are the industry standard for broilers, growing rapidly and producing a large amount of meat in a short period. Plymouth Rocks are another good option, offering a balance of decent egg production and quality meat, making them versatile for various needs.

For those seeking a dual-purpose breed that provides both eggs and meat, the Sussex or Wyandotte are suitable options. Sussex chickens are known for their friendly nature, good egg production, and quality meat. Wyandottes are also popular for their hardiness, attractive appearance, and reliable production of both eggs and meat.

Climate and environmental conditions are critical factors to consider when choosing a breed. If you live in a colder climate, breeds like the Orpington or Brahma are ideal due to their cold-hardiness. Orpingtons are large, friendly birds that lay well even in colder conditions, while Brahmas are also well-suited to cold climates, known for their size and feathered legs that provide extra warmth.

Your space and environment should also influence your decision. Some breeds thrive in free-ranging conditions, while others do well in confined spaces. For instance, breeds like the Leghorn are active and do well when allowed to forage freely, while others like the Australorp can adapt well to confinement.

Ultimately, the key to success is researching and matching the breed characteristics to your specific needs and local conditions. By considering factors such as egg and meat production, climate hardiness, and space requirements, you can choose a breed that will thrive in your environment and meet your expectations effectively.

UNDERSTANDING CHICKEN BEHAVIOR AND SOCIAL STRUCTURE

Understanding chicken behavior and their social structure is essential for maintaining a healthy and happy flock. Chickens are inherently social creatures that establish a "pecking order," which is a hierarchical system determining the social standing of each bird within the flock. This pecking order plays a crucial role in maintaining order and reducing conflicts. Typically, the dominant chicken enjoys first access to food and the best roosting spots, while subordinate chickens respect this hierarchy to maintain harmony.

Observing your chickens' behavior offers valuable insights into their health and overall well-being. Healthy chickens are typically active and curious, engaging in natural behaviors such as foraging, dust bathing, and socializing. Foraging allows chickens to express their natural instincts, as they scratch and peck at the ground in search of food. Dust bathing is another critical behavior where chickens roll in loose dirt or sand, which helps them clean their feathers and deter parasites. Socializing includes various interactions, from gentle pecking and grooming to more assertive displays of dominance.

Conversely, signs of distress or illness in chickens can manifest in various ways. Lethargy is a common symptom, where a normally active chicken becomes unusually sluggish. Isolation from the flock is another red flag; a healthy chicken generally seeks the company of its peers, so a bird that consistently stays apart may be unwell. Changes in eating and drinking habits, such as a reduced appetite or increased thirst, can also indicate health issues.

To promote positive behavior and a harmonious environment, providing ample space is crucial. Overcrowding can lead to stress and increased aggression as chickens compete for limited resources. Ensuring that each bird has enough room to move, forage, and roost comfortably helps minimize these conflicts. Similarly, providing sufficient food and water reduces competition and ensures all chickens have access to the essentials they need to thrive.

Enriching their environment is another effective strategy to keep chickens mentally and physically stimulated. Perches allow chickens to engage in their natural roosting behavior, offering a sense of security. Dust baths should be readily available, as they are vital for chickens' hygiene and comfort. Foraging opportunities can be enhanced by scattering food or introducing new objects for them to explore and peck at.

Regularly monitoring the flock for signs of bullying or aggression is also essential. Bullying can lead to injury and stress, disrupting the social harmony of the flock. Address these issues promptly by identifying the aggressor and, if necessary, providing additional resources or temporarily separating the problematic bird to allow it to reintegrate more peacefully.

CHAPTER TWO

PLANNING AND PREPARATION

ASSESSING YOUR SPACE AND RESOURCES

Before starting of raising chickens, it is crucial to carefully evaluate the space and resources available to ensure the well-being of your feathered friends. Proper planning and assessment will not only provide a comfortable environment for the chickens but also help you comply with local regulations and make informed decisions regarding their care.

Firstly, consider the space requirements for chickens. These birds need adequate room to move about, scratch for food, and nest comfortably. For the coop, each chicken should ideally have 3-4 square feet of space. This area is where they will sleep, lay eggs, and seek shelter from the elements. Additionally, outdoor run areas should provide 8-10 square feet per chicken to allow them to exercise and explore. Providing sufficient space ensures that the chickens remain healthy and reduces the risk of stress-related behaviors.

Secondly, zoning laws and regulations play a critical role in determining whether you can keep chickens on your property. Local ordinances may impose restrictions on the number of chickens you can keep, the type of coop structure allowed, and even where the coop can be located relative to your property boundaries or neighbors. It is essential to thoroughly research these regulations to avoid potential fines or legal issues down the road. Some areas may also require permits or inspections before you can start keeping chickens.

Thirdly, assess the resources available on your property. Access to a clean water source is vital for the chickens' hydration and overall health. Consider how you will provide fresh water daily, especially during hot weather. Electricity may be necessary for lighting inside the coop, particularly during shorter daylight hours or in colder climates where supplemental heating is needed. Evaluate whether your property has access to these utilities or if alternative solutions are required.

Furthermore, gather the necessary supplies for keeping chickens. This includes suitable feeders and drinkers, nesting boxes for egg-laying, bedding materials such as straw or wood shavings, and fencing to secure the outdoor run area. Having these items on hand before bringing chickens home ensures a smooth transition and minimizes stress for both you and the birds.

Lastly, consider the climate and environmental factors specific to your region. Chickens are adaptable creatures, but extremes in temperature or weather conditions can impact their health. Plan accordingly by providing adequate ventilation in the coop for airflow during warmer months and insulation for heat retention in colder months.

CREATING A CHICKEN-FRIENDLY ENVIRONMENT

Creating a chicken-friendly environment is essential for ensuring the well-being and productivity of your flock. Chickens, like any animals, thrive when their natural behaviors are supported and when they feel safe and comfortable in their surroundings. Here's a comprehensive guide on how to create an optimal chicken-friendly space:

Safety

The safety of your chickens is paramount. Predators such as foxes, raccoons, and neighborhood dogs pose significant threats. To protect your flock, start by securing the perimeter with sturdy fencing. Chicken wire is commonly used, but it's crucial to ensure it's of adequate strength and buried slightly underground to prevent digging predators. Additionally, consider reinforcing vulnerable areas with hardware cloth, which offers greater protection against determined predators. A well-designed coop with secure doors and windows is essential for nighttime safety, providing a sanctuary where chickens can rest without fear of nocturnal predators.

Shelter

Adequate shelter is crucial to protect chickens from the elements. A well-built coop provides a safe haven from extreme temperatures, drafts, rain, and wind. Ensure the coop is well-ventilated to prevent the buildup of moisture and ammonia, which can lead to respiratory issues. Good ventilation also helps regulate temperature, keeping the chickens comfortable year-round. The coop should have nesting boxes for laying eggs and roosting bars where chickens can perch at night. Clean bedding such as straw or wood shavings should be regularly replaced to maintain hygiene and prevent disease.

Foraging and Roaming

Chickens are natural foragers and enjoy scratching and pecking for insects, seeds, and plants. Designate a spacious outdoor area where chickens can roam freely during the day. This space should be securely fenced to protect them from predators and provide them with opportunities to exercise and exhibit natural behaviors. Consider implementing rotational grazing if space allows, where chickens can access different sections of pasture over time. Rotational grazing not only supports their dietary needs but also helps prevent overgrazing and promotes the regeneration of vegetation.

Additional Considerations In addition to safety, shelter, and foraging opportunities, there are several other considerations to keep in mind when creating a chicken-friendly environment:

1. Clean Water and Feeding Stations: Provide clean water in a stable container that cannot be easily tipped over. Feed should be placed in feeders that keep it dry and free from contamination. Consider using feeders that minimize waste and allow easy access for chickens.

2. Dust Bathing Areas: Chickens engage in dust bathing to maintain feather health and control parasites. Provide a designated area filled with fine dust or sand where chickens can indulge in this natural behavior.

3. Perches and Enrichment: Install various perches and objects for

enrichment inside the coop and in the outdoor area. Perches should be of different heights and thicknesses to accommodate all chickens comfortably.

4. Routine Maintenance: Regularly inspect the coop and fencing for signs of wear and tear. Clean the coop regularly to maintain hygiene and prevent disease outbreaks.

DESIGNING AND BUILDING A COOP

Designing and constructing a chicken coop is a crucial aspect of raising poultry, ensuring they have a safe and comfortable environment to thrive in. A well-planned coop serves as their sanctuary, providing spaces for nesting, roosting, and shelter from the elements.

Here's a comprehensive guide on designing and building a functional chicken coop.

Size and Layout

The size of your chicken coop directly impacts the well-being of your flock. Adequate space is essential to prevent overcrowding, which can lead to stress and health issues. A general guideline is to provide at least 2-4 square feet per chicken inside the coop, with additional space in the outdoor run area.

Consider the layout carefully to optimize functionality. Include nesting boxes for egg-laying, ensuring there's one box for every 3-4 hens to minimize competition. Position these boxes in a quiet, secluded area to encourage broodiness. Install roosting perches higher than the nesting boxes, as chickens naturally prefer to roost in elevated spots during the night. Easy access for cleaning is another critical aspect of the coop's design. Incorporate large doors or hatches that allow you to reach every corner of the coop easily. This facilitates regular cleaning, which is crucial for maintaining a healthy environment and preventing disease.

Ventilation

Proper ventilation is essential for maintaining good air quality inside the coop. Ammonia buildup from chicken droppings can be harmful to their respiratory health if not properly ventilated. Install vents near the top of the coop to ensure adequate airflow. These vents should be adjustable to control airflow depending on weather conditions, such as closing them during cold or rainy days.

Ventilation not only removes stale air and moisture but also helps regulate the temperature inside the coop, preventing overheating in summer and minimizing condensation in winter. Good airflow also discourages the growth of mold and mildew, which can thrive in damp environments.

Materials

Choosing the right materials is crucial for the durability and functionality of the chicken coop. Wood is a popular choice due to its insulation properties and natural aesthetic. Opt for sturdy, weather-resistant wood such as cedar or pressure-treated pine, which is treated to resist moisture and pests.

Ensure all wood surfaces are smooth to prevent injury to chickens and facilitate cleaning. Consider using galvanized or stainless steel hardware to prevent rusting over time. The roof should be waterproof and sloped to allow rainwater runoff.

For flooring, use materials that are easy to clean and sanitize, such as linoleum or concrete covered with a layer of bedding material like straw or wood shavings. This not only provides comfort but also absorbs moisture and odors.

ESSENTIAL TOOLS AND EQUIPMENT

Caring for chickens requires having the right tools and equipment on hand to ensure their well-being and productivity. Whether you're a seasoned poultry keeper or just starting out, preparing with essential items is crucial for maintaining a healthy and thriving flock.

Feeders and Waterers

First and foremost, providing adequate feeders and waterers is essential. Feeders should be designed to protect feed from pests and weather elements, ensuring that your chickens always have access to clean and dry food. Waterers should also be kept clean to provide a constant supply of fresh water, which is crucial for their hydration and overall health.

Cleaning Supplies

Regular maintenance of the coop is vital for the health of your chickens. Equip yourself with cleaning tools such as a rake, shovel, and broom to manage droppings, bedding, and general debris effectively. Keeping the coop clean not only prevents disease but also creates a comfortable environment for your birds to thrive in.

Health Supplies

Maintaining chicken health requires having basic medical supplies readily available. A well-stocked first aid kit is indispensable for treating minor injuries and addressing health issues promptly.

Additionally, supplements and vitamins may be necessary to support their immune systems and overall well-being, especially during periods of stress or illness.

Lighting and Heating

Environmental factors like lighting and heating play a significant role in chicken care, particularly in regions with varying climates. Supplemental lighting can stimulate egg production during shorter daylight hours, ensuring a consistent supply of eggs year-round. In colder climates, heating options for the coop may be necessary to keep chickens comfortable and prevent frostbite or other cold-related health issues during harsh winters.

By preparing these essential tools and equipment, you're not only safeguarding the health of your chickens but also setting yourself up for success as a poultry keeper. Each item serves a specific purpose in ensuring that your flock remains healthy, comfortable, and productive throughout the seasons.

CHAPTER THREE

ACQUIRING YOUR CHICKENS

SOURCING YOUR CHICKENS

When considering acquiring chickens, you have several avenues to explore: hatcheries, breeders, or rescues, each offering distinct advantages and considerations.

Hatcheries specialize in hatching and selling chicks, providing a broad selection of breeds that can be conveniently shipped directly to your location. They are particularly favored by beginners due to their accessibility and the option to purchase chicks in smaller quantities. Researching hatcheries is crucial to ensure they uphold standards of quality and humane practices. This approach is ideal for those starting out in poultry keeping, offering a reliable source of diverse breeds tailored to different needs and preferences.

Breeders, whether individuals or businesses, focus on specific chicken breeds, offering a more personalized service compared to hatcheries. They often possess in-depth knowledge of the breeds they raise, making them a valuable resource for selecting chickens based on desired traits or characteristics. Choosing to support local breeders can foster community connections and may provide opportunities to learn from experienced enthusiasts. However, availability of breeds through breeders can be more limited than what hatcheries typically offer.

Rescues present an alternative route to acquiring chickens, focusing on rehoming birds in need. These organizations often take in chickens from various situations, such as neglect or relinquishment by previous owners. Adopting from a rescue not only provides a home for chickens in need but also contributes to animal welfare efforts. Before adopting, it's important to assess the health and condition of the chickens to ensure they are suitable for integration into your flock. This option appeals to those with a commitment to animal welfare and a desire to provide a second chance to birds in distressing circumstances.

Each sourcing method comes with its own set of considerations beyond the initial acquisition. Hatchery-raised chicks require careful brooding and acclimatization to their new environment. Working with breeders may involve ongoing support and guidance as you integrate their chickens into your existing flock. Rescue chickens may require additional care to address any health or behavioral issues resulting from their previous circumstances. Regardless of the source, responsible chicken ownership involves understanding the specific needs of your chosen breeds or individuals and providing appropriate housing, nutrition, and healthcare.

Moreover, the decision of where to source your chickens can align with broader values such as sustainability, supporting local businesses, or contributing to animal welfare initiatives. Engaging with hatcheries, breeders, or rescues involves not just acquiring chickens but also becoming part of a community dedicated to poultry care and husbandry. Whether you're drawn to the diversity offered by hatcheries, the expertise of breeders, or the compassionate mission of rescues, each option represents a pathway into the fulfilling world of chicken keeping, where thoughtful consideration and responsible stewardship play vital roles in the well-being of these feathered companions.

WHAT TO LOOK FOR WHEN BUYING CHICKS OR MATURE BIRDS

When starting on the journey of acquiring chickens, whether as chicks or mature birds, there are several crucial factors to carefully consider. These considerations can significantly impact the health, productivity, and overall satisfaction you derive from your poultry.

Firstly, the health and vitality of the birds should be a top priority. Opt for chickens that display vigor, with bright eyes, clean feathers, and active behavior. Avoid any signs of lethargy, nasal discharge, or visible injuries, as these could indicate underlying health issues that might affect the longevity and productivity of your flock.

Understanding the breed characteristics is equally essential. Different breeds offer distinct advantages depending on your specific goals. For instance, if you prioritize high egg production, breeds like Leghorns or Rhode Island Reds might be suitable choices. On the other hand, if you seek chickens with a docile temperament for backyard companionship, Brahmas or Orpingtons could be more appropriate. Consider factors such as climate adaptability, as some breeds are better suited to cold or hot climates than others.

Age plays a crucial role in your decision-making process. Chicks, typically under 8 weeks old, require careful attention and specific care to ensure they grow into healthy adults. They are ideal if you want to experience the joy of raising chickens from a young age and imprinting them with good husbandry practices. Conversely, mature birds offer the advantage of immediate egg production or readiness for breeding, depending on your goals and experience level with poultry care.

Sexing is another critical consideration, especially if you have specific plans for your flock. Determining the sex of chicks accurately can be challenging, but it's essential if you aim to maintain a flock primarily for egg-laying purposes, as roosters are unnecessary in such scenarios. Alternatively, purchasing pullets (young hens) ensures you start with birds already confirmed to be females, saving you the effort and potential complications associated with sexing.

Documentation is often overlooked but can be vital, especially if you intend to participate in shows or breed your chickens. Requesting vaccination records and pedigree information ensures you start with birds that have received necessary health protections and come from reputable breeding stock. This documentation not only safeguards the health of your flock but also enhances the value of your chickens if you decide to expand into breeding or showing poultry.

TRANSPORTATION AND INITIAL SETUP

Transporting and setting up chickens properly is essential for ensuring their health and well-being from the moment you acquire them. This process involves careful planning and attention to detail to minimize stress and create a safe environment for your new feathered friends.

Transportation: Transporting chickens requires a gentle approach to minimize stress and potential injury. Before transporting them, ensure you have a suitable carrier that provides adequate ventilation and protection from the elements. This could be a well-ventilated crate or a specially designed transport box. Make sure the carrier is clean and free from any sharp edges that could harm the chickens during transit.

When handling chickens, always do so with care. Catch them calmly and securely, supporting their bodies to prevent unnecessary flapping or struggling. Transport them in a way that minimizes jostling and sudden movements, which can agitate them. If the journey is long, consider providing some bedding material to absorb droppings and make the journey more comfortable.

Initial Setup: Preparing their new living space before bringing chickens home is crucial. A secure coop or housing is necessary to protect them from predators and adverse weather conditions. The coop should be well-built, with sturdy walls and a predator-proof design. Check for any gaps or openings that predators could exploit, and reinforce or repair them as needed.

Inside the coop, provide suitable bedding such as straw, wood shavings, or shredded paper. This will help keep the chickens comfortable and provide insulation. Ensure there are separate areas for feeding, drinking, and nesting. Install perches at different heights for the chickens to roost comfortably, as they naturally prefer elevated positions for sleeping.

Food and water should be easily accessible and placed in locations where chickens can access them without difficulty. Use feeders and waterers designed for poultry to keep food clean and prevent spillage. Provide a balanced diet appropriate for their age and breed, which typically includes a mix of grains, pellets, and greens.

Acclimatization: Allow your chickens time to acclimate to their new surroundings. Moving to a new environment can be stressful for them, so observe their behavior closely during the initial days. Ensure they are eating, drinking, and behaving normally.

Monitor their health, checking for signs of illness such as lethargy, unusual droppings, or respiratory issues.

During this period, limit disturbances and interactions with the chickens to help them settle in peacefully. Gradually introduce them to their outdoor space if they will have access to a run or free-range area. This gradual introduction allows them to familiarize themselves with their new surroundings while feeling secure in their coop.

☐

CHAPTER FOUR

FEEDING AND NUTRITION

UNDERSTANDING CHICKEN DIETARY NEEDS

Understanding the dietary requirements of chickens is crucial for ensuring their health and productivity. Chickens, like all living creatures, need a balanced diet that includes proteins, carbohydrates, fats, vitamins, and minerals. The specific proportions of these nutrients can vary based on factors such as the chicken's age, breed, and purpose, whether they are raised for egg production, meat, or both.

Chicks, particularly in their early stages of development, require higher levels of protein to support rapid growth. Protein is essential for building muscle and tissue, which is critical during the chick's initial stages of life. As chicks mature into adulthood, their protein needs may decrease slightly, but it remains an important component of their diet throughout their lives.

In addition to protein, carbohydrates serve as an important energy source for chickens. Carbohydrates are primarily derived from grains and provide the necessary energy for various bodily functions and activities, including movement and egg production in laying hens.

Fats are another vital component of a chicken's diet, serving as a concentrated source of energy. Fats help maintain healthy skin and feathers and aid in the absorption of fat-soluble vitamins. However, excessive fat intake can lead to obesity and other health issues, so it's important to balance fat levels appropriately in the diet.

Vitamins and minerals play essential roles in maintaining overall health and preventing deficiencies. Vitamins such as A, D, E, and K are necessary for proper growth, immunity, and reproductive health in chickens. Minerals like calcium, phosphorus, and magnesium are crucial for bone development, eggshell formation, and muscle function.

To ensure chickens receive the necessary nutrients, many poultry owners opt to use commercial chicken feeds. These feeds are formulated to meet the specific nutritional requirements of chickens at different stages of life and production. They typically contain a balanced mixture of grains, protein sources (such as soybean meal or fish meal), vitamins, and minerals. Choosing a high-quality commercial feed can simplify the process of providing adequate nutrition to chickens.

Alternatively, some poultry owners prefer to create homemade chicken feeds. This approach allows for more control over the ingredients and can be tailored to meet specific dietary needs or preferences. Homemade feeds often include a combination of grains (such as corn, wheat, and oats), protein sources (like peas or mealworms), and supplements to ensure a well-rounded diet.

Regardless of whether you choose commercial feeds or homemade mixes, it's essential to regularly assess your chickens' dietary needs. Factors such as environmental conditions, seasonal changes, and individual health considerations can influence nutrient requirements. Monitoring the birds' growth, egg production (if applicable), and overall condition can provide valuable insights into the adequacy of their diet.

TYPES OF CHICKEN FEED

Chicken feed plays a crucial role in the health and productivity of poultry, with different types formulated to meet specific nutritional needs at various stages of their life cycle. Understanding these distinctions enables poultry owners to provide optimal care and support for their flock.

Starter Feeds

Starter feeds are essential for newly hatched chicks, providing them with the necessary nutrients to support rapid growth and development during their early weeks of life. These feeds are typically high in protein to promote muscle and skeletal development, as well as vitamins and minerals crucial for overall health. Young chicks require a diet that supports their fragile immune systems and prepares them for the transition to solid foods.

Grower Feeds

As chicks mature into adolescent chickens, they transition to grower feeds. These feeds are designed to provide a balanced diet that supports steady growth and development without promoting excessive weight gain. Grower feeds continue to emphasize protein but adjust the nutrient ratios to accommodate the changing needs of growing chickens. The goal is to ensure healthy bone development and proper feather growth as they approach adulthood.

Layer Feeds

Layer feeds are specifically formulated for hens that are actively laying eggs. These feeds are enriched with calcium to support the production of strong eggshells, which is crucial for maintaining egg quality and preventing issues like thin shells or breakage. Layer feeds also contain balanced levels of protein, vitamins, and minerals to support overall health and sustain egg production over extended periods.

Broiler Feeds

Broiler feeds are tailored for chickens raised for meat production. These feeds are formulated to promote efficient growth and muscle development, ensuring that broilers reach market weight in a relatively short period. They typically contain higher levels of protein and energy compared to feeds for layers or growers, reflecting the accelerated growth requirements of meat-producing chickens.

Each type of chicken feed is carefully formulated to meet specific nutritional requirements, taking into account factors such as age, purpose (egg-laying or meat production), and overall health considerations. For instance, supplements or special formulations might be necessary in certain circumstances, such as during molting or in regions with specific dietary deficiencies in local feed sources.

Understanding the nutritional needs of chickens at different stages of their life cycle is essential for maintaining flock health and optimizing productivity. Poultry owners should consult with poultry nutritionists or veterinarians to ensure they are selecting the appropriate feeds and making any necessary adjustments based on local conditions or specific health concerns within their flock.

By choosing the right feed for their chickens, owners can help ensure that their poultry not only survives but thrives, whether they are raising them for eggs, meat, or simply as beloved backyard companions. Proper nutrition lays the foundation for healthy, happy chickens and contributes to the sustainability and success of poultry operations worldwide.

SUPPLEMENTS AND TREATS

Supplements and treats play a pivotal role in enhancing the diet of chickens, complementing the nutrition provided by commercial feeds. While commercial feeds are designed to meet most of a chicken's nutritional needs, supplements and treats offer additional benefits that contribute to overall health and well-being.

Firstly, supplements are valuable additions to a chicken's diet. Calcium supplements, for instance, are crucial for maintaining strong bones and eggshell quality. Chickens that have access to calcium supplements, such as crushed oyster shells or calcium carbonate, are better equipped to lay eggs with durable shells, reducing the likelihood of shell deformities or breakage. This is particularly important for laying hens, as egg production places significant demands on their calcium reserves.

Another essential supplement is grit, which aids in digestion. Chickens do not have teeth and rely on grit—small stones or insoluble minerals—to grind their food in the gizzard. This grinding action helps break down food into smaller particles, making it easier for the digestive enzymes to extract nutrients. Without sufficient grit, chickens may struggle to digest their food properly, leading to digestive issues and nutrient deficiencies.

In addition to supplements, treats serve as a source of enrichment and supplementary nutrition for chickens. Treats can include a variety of foods such as fruits, vegetables, and insects like mealworms. These treats not only diversify the chicken's diet but also provide vitamins, minerals, and other nutrients that may not be present in sufficient quantities in commercial feeds alone.

Fruits such as berries or apples offer vitamins and antioxidants, while vegetables like leafy greens or carrots provide essential vitamins and fiber.

Mealworms and other insects are rich in protein, which is crucial for muscle development and overall health, especially for growing chicks or during molting periods when protein requirements are higher.

However, it is crucial to offer treats in moderation. While treats can be beneficial, excessive amounts can lead to nutritional imbalances and obesity in chickens. Obesity in poultry can result in a range of health issues, including joint problems and reduced egg production. Therefore, treats should be given sparingly and ideally as a supplement to a balanced diet of commercial feed.

Moreover, the quality of treats matters. Fresh, organic fruits and vegetables are preferable over processed or sugary treats, which offer little nutritional value and can potentially harm the chickens' health if consumed in excess. Careful selection and moderation ensure that treats enhance rather than detract from the overall nutritional balance of the chicken's diet.

FEEDING PRACTICES AND SCHEDULES

Establishing proper feeding practices and schedules is crucial for the health, productivity, and overall well-being of your flock. Consistency, cleanliness, adequate quantity, vigilant monitoring, effective feeding systems, and ample water supply are key components to consider.

Consistency is vital in feeding practices. Chickens thrive on routine, so feeding them at the same time every day helps create a predictable schedule. This regularity reduces stress among the flock as they learn when to expect their meals. Stress reduction is important because stressed chickens are more prone to illness and lower productivity. Cleanliness cannot be overstated in poultry management. Always provide fresh feed and ensure that water is clean. Dirty or moldy feed can lead to numerous health problems, including infections and digestive issues. Similarly, water must be clean and fresh to prevent diseases and ensure proper hydration. Regularly clean and disinfect feeders and waterers to maintain a hygienic environment.

Quantity of feed is another critical factor. Each chicken must have access to enough feed, which means preventing overcrowding at feeders. Overcrowding can result in weaker birds being pushed away and deprived of necessary nutrition. Ensure that the feeding area is spacious enough for all chickens to eat comfortably at the same time. This not only ensures equitable distribution of food but also minimizes aggression and competition among birds.

Monitoring the flock's health and behavior is essential to maintain optimal feeding practices. Keep a close watch on the weight, behavior, and overall health of your chickens. Regular checks will help you identify any issues early, allowing you to adjust their diet as needed. For instance, if you notice a decline in the quality of eggs or meat, it may indicate a need for dietary adjustments. Additionally, observe how much feed is being consumed. Sudden changes in feed intake can be a sign of health problems.

Feeding systems should be designed to minimize waste and prevent contamination. Traditional feeders can lead to significant food waste and contamination. Consider using hanging feeders or automatic feeders, which can be more efficient. Hanging feeders are elevated, preventing chickens from scratching and contaminating the feed, while automatic feeders ensure a consistent supply of food and reduce waste.

Water is just as important as feed. Chickens need a constant supply of clean, fresh water to stay hydrated and digest their food properly. This is especially crucial in hot weather when chickens are more prone to dehydration. Waterers should be cleaned regularly and checked multiple times a day to ensure they are functioning correctly. Automatic waterers can be a convenient option, providing a steady supply of fresh water.

☐

CHAPTER FIVE

HEALTH AND WELLNESS

COMMON CHICKEN DISEASES AND HOW TO PREVENT THEM

Chickens are susceptible to a variety of diseases, which can significantly impact their health and productivity. Understanding these diseases and implementing preventive measures is crucial for maintaining a healthy flock. Here, we discuss some of the most common chicken diseases and effective ways to prevent them.

Marek's Disease

Marek's Disease is a highly contagious viral infection that affects chickens, causing tumors and paralysis. It is caused by the herpesvirus and primarily affects young birds. Infected chickens may show symptoms such as weight loss, irregular pupils, and leg paralysis. Unfortunately, once a chicken is infected, there is no cure. The most effective prevention method is vaccination. Chicks should be vaccinated within the first day of life to ensure immunity against this debilitating disease.

Newcastle Disease

Newcastle Disease is another highly contagious viral infection that impacts the respiratory, nervous, and digestive systems of chickens. Symptoms include coughing, sneezing, greenish diarrhea, and twisting of the neck. The virus spreads rapidly through direct contact with infected birds, contaminated feed, and equipment. Vaccination is essential for prevention, along with maintaining strict hygiene practices. Ensuring that the coop and surrounding areas are clean, and isolating new or sick birds can help control the spread of this disease.

Avian Influenza

Commonly known as bird flu, Avian Influenza is a viral infection that can be deadly to chickens. Symptoms vary from mild to severe and can include respiratory distress, swollen sinuses, and decreased egg production. This disease can spread through wild birds, contaminated water, and equipment. Preventive measures include vaccinating the flock, keeping wild birds away from the coop, and maintaining cleanliness. Regularly disinfecting the coop and equipment, and ensuring good biosecurity practices can significantly reduce the risk of an outbreak.

Fowl Pox

Fowl Pox is a viral disease that causes lesions on a chicken's skin and inside their mouth. It spreads through direct contact or via mosquitoes. Symptoms include wart-like sores on the comb, wattles, and beak, which can hinder feeding and breathing. Vaccination is the best preventive measure against Fowl Pox. Additionally, controlling the mosquito population around the coop and maintaining good sanitation practices can help prevent the spread of the virus.

Coccidiosis

Coccidiosis is a parasitic disease caused by protozoa that affects the intestines of chickens. It is characterized by symptoms such as diarrhea, poor growth, and lethargy. The disease spreads through the ingestion of infected feces, often present in contaminated water or feed. Preventive measures include maintaining good sanitation, providing medicated feed, and ensuring dry, clean living conditions. Regularly cleaning the coop, feeding areas, and water containers can help reduce the risk of infection.

General Prevention Tips

Preventing these diseases primarily involves maintaining a clean environment, providing a balanced diet, and ensuring your chickens are vaccinated against common diseases. Regular cleaning of the coop, feeding areas, and water containers is essential. Isolate new birds before introducing them to the flock and watch for any signs of illness. Keeping the living area dry and well-ventilated also helps in reducing the risk of infections. Proper nutrition strengthens the chickens' immune system, making them more resilient to diseases.

REGULAR HEALTH CHECKS AND GROOMING

Maintaining the health and well-being of your chickens is paramount, and regular health checks coupled with consistent grooming practices play a crucial role in ensuring their vitality. Here's an in-depth guide on how to conduct these health checks and grooming routines effectively.

Daily Observation

Daily observation is the cornerstone of preventative health care for your flock. Spend a few minutes each day watching your chickens closely. Pay attention to any changes in their behavior, appetite, or appearance. Healthy chickens are usually active, have a good appetite, and display smooth, glossy feathers. Signs of potential issues include lethargy, reduced appetite, drooping wings, or abnormal feather condition. Early detection through daily observation can help address problems before they escalate.

Weekly Physical Checks

In addition to daily observation, conduct a thorough physical check of each chicken on a weekly basis. Handle your chickens gently but thoroughly to inspect for any external parasites such as mites and lice. These parasites can cause significant discomfort and health problems if left untreated. Also, check for any injuries, signs of illness, or abnormalities in their overall body condition. Look for swellings, cuts, or unusual lumps that might indicate underlying health issues. Regular handling helps chickens get accustomed to being checked and makes it easier to spot any changes.

Beak and Claw Maintenance

Chickens' beaks and claws naturally wear down as they peck and scratch, but sometimes they can overgrow, leading to discomfort and difficulty in feeding or walking. Ensure that your chickens have access to hard surfaces like rocks or rough perches, which can help them maintain their beaks and claws at a proper length. If you notice overgrowth, you might need to trim them. Use specialized poultry nail clippers or consult a veterinarian if you're unsure how to trim them safely. Regular maintenance prevents overgrowth-related issues and ensures your chickens can forage and move comfortably.

Feather Care

Healthy feathers are a good indicator of a chicken's overall well-being. Feathers should be clean and shiny. During your weekly checks, inspect your chickens for signs of molting or feather loss. Molting is a natural process where chickens shed old feathers and grow new ones, but excessive feather loss outside of molting periods can indicate stress, poor nutrition, or health problems. Ensure your chickens have a balanced diet rich in proteins and access to clean water to support healthy feather growth.

__Dust Baths__

Grooming is an essential aspect of maintaining hygiene and noticing abnormalities early. Chickens naturally keep their feathers clean and free of parasites by taking dust baths. Provide an area with loose, dry soil or sand where your chickens can bathe. Dust baths help them control external parasites like mites and lice and keep their feathers in optimal condition. Regular access to dust baths is essential for their comfort and health.

DEALING WITH INJURIES AND ILLNESSES

Despite providing the best care, chickens can sometimes get injured or fall ill. Being prepared and knowing how to handle these situations can make a significant difference in their recovery and overall well-being. Here's a comprehensive guide on dealing with common chicken health issues, focusing on injuries, respiratory problems, and digestive issues.

Handling Injuries

Chickens can sustain minor cuts or wounds from various sources, such as sharp objects, pecking, or predator attacks. When you notice an injury, it's crucial to act promptly to prevent infection and promote healing. Here's a step-by-step approach:

1. Cleaning the Wound: Gently clean the affected area with an antiseptic

solution. This helps remove any dirt and bacteria that could lead to infection.

2.   Monitoring for Infection: Keep a close eye on the wound for signs of infection, such as redness, swelling, or discharge. If these symptoms appear, further medical treatment may be necessary.

3.   Isolation: Separate the injured bird from the rest of the flock. This prevents other chickens from pecking at the wound, which could exacerbate the injury and delay healing.

Having a basic first aid kit for your chickens can be extremely beneficial. Essential items to include are antiseptic solutions, bandages, and tools like eye droppers for administering medication.

Addressing Respiratory Issues

Respiratory problems in chickens can manifest through symptoms such as coughing, sneezing, and nasal discharge. These issues can arise from various causes, including poor ventilation, dust, and infections. Here's how to manage respiratory problems:

1.   Ensure Proper Ventilation: Good airflow in the coop is vital. Poor ventilation can lead to the buildup of ammonia from droppings, which irritates the respiratory tract.

2.   Observe and Act: Monitor your chickens for persistent symptoms. If coughing, sneezing, or nasal discharge continues, it's important to seek

veterinary advice. Early intervention can prevent more serious health issues.

Maintaining a clean and well-ventilated living environment significantly reduces the risk of respiratory problems. Regularly cleaning the coop and ensuring it's not overcrowded are proactive steps in promoting respiratory health.

Managing Digestive Problems

Digestive issues in chickens, such as diarrhea, can stem from a variety of causes, including dietary changes, infections, or parasites. Effective management involves:

1. Maintaining Clean Water: Ensure your chickens always have access to clean, fresh water. Contaminated water

can be a significant source of digestive problems.

2. Providing a Balanced Diet: A balanced diet tailored to the specific nutritional needs of chickens is essential. Abrupt changes in diet can upset their digestive system, so any dietary adjustments should be gradual.

3. Veterinary Consultation: Persistent diarrhea or other signs of digestive distress warrant a consultation with a veterinarian. They can provide accurate diagnoses and appropriate treatments, such as medications or dietary adjustments.

Regular monitoring of your chickens' droppings can help detect early signs of digestive issues, allowing for timely intervention.

VACCINATION AND BIOSECURITY MEASURES

Vaccination and biosecurity measures are crucial for maintaining the health of your flock. Vaccination helps protect your chickens against common diseases, while biosecurity practices prevent the introduction and spread of illnesses. Here's a detailed guide to help you keep your chickens healthy and productive through these essential practices.

Vaccination

Consult a Veterinarian: To determine the appropriate vaccines for your chickens, it's essential to consult a veterinarian. A vet can provide tailored advice based on your location and the specific disease threats in your area. Some common vaccines include those for Marek's disease, Newcastle disease, and fowl pox. Each of these diseases poses significant risks to poultry, and vaccination is a key preventive measure.

Follow a Vaccination Schedule: Adhering to a vaccination schedule is crucial. Vaccines are most effective when administered at the correct times, typically beginning when chicks are just a few days old. For example, Marek's disease vaccine is usually given to day-old chicks, while Newcastle disease and fowl pox vaccines have their specific schedules. Your veterinarian can provide a comprehensive vaccination plan to ensure your chickens are protected from the start.

Quarantine New Birds: Introducing new birds to your existing flock can bring in diseases. To mitigate this risk, always quarantine new chickens for at least two weeks before integrating them with your flock. During this period, monitor the new birds for any signs of illness. Quarantine helps prevent the spread of potential diseases to your healthy chickens, safeguarding the entire flock.

Limit Visitors: Reducing the number of people and animals that come into contact with your chickens is another important biosecurity measure. Visitors can unknowingly carry pathogens on their clothes, shoes, or equipment, posing a risk to your flock. By minimizing access, you reduce the chances of disease transmission. When visitors are necessary, ensure they follow strict hygiene practices.

Clean Footwear and Tools: Pathogens can easily be transported into your chicken area on footwear and tools. Implement a protocol for cleaning and disinfecting shoes and equipment before they enter the chicken zone. Providing footbaths or disposable shoe covers can be effective in preventing the introduction of harmful pathogens. Similarly, ensure that tools used in the chicken area are regularly cleaned and sanitized.

Regular Monitoring and Good Hygiene

Consistent monitoring of your flock is essential. Observe your chickens daily for any signs of illness, such as lethargy, changes in eating habits, or unusual behavior. Early detection of disease allows for prompt treatment and can prevent the spread of illness within your flock.

Maintaining good hygiene is also critical. Regularly clean the chicken coop, nesting boxes, and feeding areas. Proper waste management helps reduce the risk of disease by minimizing the

presence of harmful bacteria and
parasites.

CHAPTER SIX

DAILY AND SEASONAL CARE

DAILY CARE ROUTINES

Daily care routines are the foundation of keeping your chickens healthy and content. Here's a straightforward guide to what you should do every day:

Feeding and Watering

Feed: Providing a balanced diet is crucial for the health of your chickens. Their diet should primarily consist of grains, pellets, or crumbles formulated to meet their nutritional needs. Incorporate fresh vegetables and occasional treats like mealworms to keep their diet varied and interesting. Always ensure that the feed is fresh and stored in a dry place to prevent mold and spoilage, which can be harmful to your chickens.

Water: Access to clean, fresh water is essential at all times. Chickens can become dehydrated quickly, especially in hot weather, so it is vital to check and refill water containers daily. Use containers that are easy to clean and less likely to be knocked over. In colder months, ensure that the water doesn't freeze.

Egg Collection

Collecting eggs daily is a necessary routine that helps maintain cleanliness and reduces the risk of eggs being broken or eaten by the hens. Regular collection also allows you to monitor the laying patterns of your chickens and ensures you can promptly identify any issues such as decreased egg production, which might indicate health problems. Use clean hands or gloves when handling eggs to minimize the risk of contamination.

Cleaning

Maintaining a clean coop is fundamental to the health of your flock. Every day, remove droppings from the coop and nesting boxes to reduce the risk of disease. Replace bedding regularly, ensuring that the environment remains dry and hygienic. Cleanliness helps prevent the buildup of ammonia from droppings, which can cause respiratory issues in chickens. Also, inspect the coop for any areas that might be damp or show signs of mold, as these conditions can lead to health problems.

Health Check

Daily health checks are essential for early detection of potential health issues. Observe your chickens for any signs of illness, such as unusual droppings, changes in behavior, or physical abnormalities. Look for symptoms like lethargy, coughing, sneezing, or discharges from the eyes or nose. Pay attention to their feathers, eyes, and legs for any signs of parasites or infections. Early detection can often prevent more serious problems and help ensure the wellbeing of your flock.

Social Interaction

Spending time with your chickens every day is beneficial for both you and the birds. Regular interaction helps your chickens become accustomed to human presence, making handling and care easier. Social chickens are generally less stressed and healthier. Use this time to observe their behavior and ensure that all members of the flock are getting along well. Socializing also gives you the opportunity to build trust with your chickens, making them more manageable and enhancing your enjoyment of keeping them.

SEASONAL ADJUSTMENTS AND CONSIDERATIONS

Caring for chickens requires adapting your routines to suit the changing seasons. Each season presents unique challenges and opportunities for maintaining the health and productivity of your flock. Here's a detailed guide on how to adjust your chicken care throughout the year:

Spring

Spring marks the breeding season, making it an ideal time for hatching chicks. To ensure the successful growth of the chicks, set up a brooder with the appropriate temperature and bedding. The brooder should be warm enough, typically starting at 95°F and decreasing by 5°F each week until it matches the ambient temperature.

Feeding is crucial in spring, especially if your hens are laying eggs. Increase the protein content in their diet to support egg production. A higher protein diet helps in the development of strong, healthy chicks and keeps the hens in good condition. Incorporate protein-rich feeds like mealworms, soybean meal, or specially formulated layer feed.

Summer

Summer brings the risk of heat stress and dehydration. To manage heat, provide ample shade and fresh, cool water throughout the day. Consider adding electrolytes to their water to help prevent dehydration. Chickens are prone to overheating, so ensure they have a cool, shaded area to retreat to during the hottest parts of the day.

Ventilation is another critical factor in summer. Ensure the coop is well-ventilated to allow hot air to escape and fresh air to circulate. This helps in maintaining a cooler environment inside the coop, preventing overheating and respiratory problems.

Autumn

In autumn, chickens go through molting, shedding old feathers and growing new ones. This process requires significant energy, so increase the protein in their diet to support feather growth. Good sources of protein include black oil sunflower seeds, fish meal, and high-quality feed.

Autumn is also the time to prepare for the upcoming winter. Inspect the coop for drafts and repair any damage to ensure it remains warm and dry. Adding extra bedding can help insulate the coop and provide additional warmth. Consider using straw or wood shavings, which are excellent insulators.

Winter

Winter care focuses on keeping your chickens warm and ensuring they have enough energy to generate body heat. Insulate the coop to retain heat, and if necessary, provide a safe heat source like a heat lamp or a heated pad designed for poultry. Be cautious with heat sources to avoid fire hazards.

Ventilation in winter is just as important as in summer, but for different reasons. Ensure there's enough ventilation to prevent moisture buildup, which can lead to respiratory issues and frostbite. However, avoid direct drafts on the chickens.

Feeding during winter should include offering warm mash or additional grains, which can help chickens maintain their body heat. Providing warm water will encourage them to drink more, as cold water might deter them from staying hydrated.

MANAGING MOLTING AND BROODINESS

Molting and broodiness are natural processes that chickens undergo, each requiring specific care and attention to ensure the health and well-being of your flock.

Molting

Molting is a natural cycle where chickens shed old feathers to make way for new growth. This typically occurs in the fall and can be a stressful time for your birds. Recognizing the signs of molting is crucial for providing the necessary care. Chickens in molt will lose feathers and often appear scruffy or unkempt. You may notice bare patches where feathers have fallen out.

During molting, chickens need a diet high in protein to support the growth of new feathers. Feathers are composed primarily of keratin, a protein, so ensuring your flock receives enough protein is vital. You can increase protein intake by providing high-protein feeds or supplements such as mealworms, fish meal, or specially formulated molting feeds available at poultry supply stores.

Minimizing stress is also essential during molting. Stress can be caused by environmental changes, predator threats, or even pecking order disputes within the flock. Keep the environment calm and stable, and ensure that chickens have a warm, safe place to roost, especially as they may be more vulnerable to the cold without their full plumage. Providing extra bedding and ensuring they are protected from drafts can help keep them comfortable.

Broodiness

Broodiness is when a hen has the instinct to sit on eggs to hatch them, often refusing to leave the nest. While this behavior is natural, it can be problematic if you do not wish to hatch chicks. Recognizing a broody hen is straightforward: she will spend most of her time in the nesting box, puffing up her feathers, and may become defensive if you try to remove her.

Managing broodiness involves several steps. If you don't want the hen to hatch eggs, remove her from the nest regularly. This helps disrupt the broody behavior. Sometimes, simply taking the hen out and placing her in a different part of the coop can break the cycle. Ensure that the nesting area is less attractive by collecting eggs frequently and keeping the nesting boxes clean.

In more persistent cases, you may need to use a broody breaker cage. This is a wire-bottomed cage that allows air to circulate around the hen, cooling her underside and helping to break the broody cycle. Place the cage in a well-lit, active area of the coop to discourage her broody behavior. Most hens will abandon broodiness after a few days in the broody breaker cage.

It's essential to monitor the health of a broody hen, as they may neglect to eat or drink adequately. Ensure she has access to food and water when out of the nest, and provide a balanced diet to maintain her health during this period.

PREDATOR PROTECTION AND SECURITY

Ensuring the safety of your chickens from predators is essential for their well-being. Here are comprehensive measures to secure their environment:

Coop Security

A robust coop is the first line of defense against predators. Construct the coop using durable materials to withstand potential attacks. Reinforce all doors and windows with secure locks to prevent unauthorized access. Instead of chicken wire, use hardware cloth for fencing. Hardware cloth is significantly stronger and more resistant to tearing or chewing by predators, providing a more reliable barrier.

Night Safety

Predators are most active at night, making it crucial to secure your chickens during these hours. Installing automatic doors is a practical solution. These doors close the coop at dusk and open it at dawn, ensuring the chickens are safely enclosed without requiring manual intervention. Additionally, use predator-proof latches and locks on all doors and windows to fortify the coop further. These locks are designed to be difficult for animals to manipulate, adding an extra layer of security.

Daytime Protection

While free-ranging during the day offers numerous benefits for chickens, it also exposes them to potential threats. Supervision is key when allowing the flock to roam freely. Alternatively, a secure run can provide a safe environment for them to explore without the risk of predator attacks. Another effective strategy is the use of guard animals. Dogs, geese, or other vigilant animals can deter predators and alert you to their presence, offering an additional protective measure for your flock.

Monitoring

Continuous monitoring is vital for maintaining the security of your chickens. Installing cameras around the coop allows you to observe any predator activity in real time. This not only helps in identifying potential threats but also in taking proactive measures to prevent future incidents. Surveillance footage can be invaluable in understanding predator behavior and adjusting your security strategies accordingly.

☐

CHAPTER SEVEN

EGG PRODUCTION AND MANAGEMENT

UNDERSTANDING EGG LAYING CYCLES

The egg-laying cycle of hens is a critical aspect of poultry farming, essential for maximizing egg production. This cycle commences when hens reach maturity, typically at 18 to 20 weeks of age. While hens can continue laying eggs for several years, their most prolific period occurs within the first 12 to 18 months. To optimize egg production during this peak phase and beyond, understanding the intricacies of the egg-laying cycle is vital.

Hens lay eggs in cycles averaging 24 to 26 hours. This cycle is influenced by various factors including the breed of the hen, its age, nutrition, and environmental conditions such as lighting. Different breeds of hens have varying egg-laying capabilities and cycles. For instance, some breeds are genetically predisposed to lay more eggs than others. Age also plays a significant role; as hens grow older, the frequency of egg-laying decreases, and the quality of eggs may decline.

Nutrition is another crucial factor impacting the egg-laying cycle. Hens require a balanced diet rich in proteins, vitamins, and minerals to maintain consistent egg production. Calcium is particularly important for the formation of strong eggshells. Inadequate calcium levels can lead to weaker shells and even affect the hen's overall health. Therefore, providing a diet supplemented with calcium-rich feeds like oyster shells or specialized poultry feed is essential.

Lighting conditions significantly influence the egg-laying cycle. Hens are naturally inclined to lay eggs when daylight is abundant. The presence of light stimulates the production of hormones that trigger egg-laying. For optimal egg production, hens need approximately 14 to 16 hours of light each day. During seasons with shorter daylight hours, artificial lighting can be used to extend the amount of light exposure. Implementing a consistent lighting schedule helps in maintaining regular laying cycles, ensuring that hens continue to produce eggs efficiently even during the winter months.

Proper management of these factors—breed selection, age, nutrition, and lighting—can lead to sustained and efficient egg production. Farmers often implement various strategies to ensure these conditions are met. For instance, selecting high-yield breeds and providing a nutrient-rich diet tailored to the hens' needs are common practices. Additionally, maintaining a controlled lighting environment with timers to simulate longer daylight hours can significantly enhance egg production.

Regular monitoring and adjustments are necessary to address any changes in the hens' laying patterns. As hens age or as environmental conditions change, farmers may need to adapt their strategies to continue achieving high levels of production. This might include adjusting the diet to address specific nutritional deficiencies or modifying the lighting setup to ensure consistent light exposure.

MAXIMIZING EGG PRODUCTION

Maximizing egg production in hens requires a multifaceted approach that focuses on providing an optimal environment and maintaining the health and well-being of the birds. Here are some key strategies to achieve this:

Nutrition

Feeding hens a balanced diet is crucial for maximizing egg production. A diet rich in proteins, vitamins, and minerals supports the hens' overall health and egg-laying capabilities. Specifically formulated layer feed is essential as it contains the appropriate nutrients tailored for egg-laying hens. Proteins are vital for egg formation, while vitamins and minerals like calcium and phosphorus are necessary for strong eggshells. It's also beneficial to provide access to oyster shells or other calcium supplements to ensure the hens get enough calcium.

Lighting

Maintaining a consistent lighting schedule is another critical factor. Hens require 14-16 hours of light daily to maintain optimal egg production, as the light stimulates their laying cycle. During shorter winter days, artificial lighting can be used to extend daylight hours. It's important to gradually adjust the lighting schedule to prevent stress. For example, increasing the light duration by about 15 minutes per week can help the hens adjust smoothly without negatively impacting their laying patterns.

Housing

Proper housing is essential for the health and productivity of hens.

Comfortable and clean housing with proper ventilation helps to reduce the risk of respiratory issues and other diseases. Each hen should have adequate space to move freely to prevent overcrowding, which can lead to stress and aggressive behavior, both of which negatively impact egg production. Providing nesting boxes is crucial as hens prefer to lay eggs in a quiet, private place. The nesting boxes should be clean and lined with soft bedding to encourage hens to use them consistently.

Health Management

Regular health checks and vaccinations are fundamental for preventing diseases that can impair egg production. Monitoring hens for signs of illness allows for early detection and prompt treatment. Parasite control, including regular deworming and mite treatments, is also essential. Parasites can cause significant health problems, leading to reduced egg production. Maintaining a clean living environment and practicing good biosecurity measures can help prevent the introduction and spread of diseases.

Stress Reduction

Minimizing stress is vital for maintaining high egg production. Hens are sensitive to stress, which can be triggered by loud noises, sudden changes in the environment, or rough handling. It's important to provide a calm and stable environment. Gentle handling and consistent routines can help reduce stress. Additionally, ensuring that hens have access to clean water and sufficient food at all times helps prevent competition and stress among the flock.

By implementing these strategies, farmers can create an environment that supports the health and productivity of their hens, leading to maximized egg production. A holistic approach that combines proper nutrition, consistent lighting, comfortable housing, diligent health management, and stress reduction is essential for achieving optimal results in egg production.

Maintaining the quality and safety of eggs from the moment they are collected until they are stored is a process that requires careful attention and proper techniques. Ensuring these practices are followed helps in preserving the eggs' freshness and minimizing the risk of contamination.

Collecting Eggs

The process begins with the timely collection of eggs. It is recommended to gather eggs at least twice daily, ideally in the early morning and late afternoon. Frequent collection helps in reducing the chances of eggs becoming dirty, cracked, or otherwise damaged. During collection, it is crucial to handle the eggs with clean hands or gloves. This practice minimizes the risk of introducing contaminants that can spoil the eggs or pose health risks.

Cleaning Eggs

Once collected, the eggs may need cleaning, especially if they have dirt or debris on their shells. The preferred method of cleaning is dry cleaning, which involves using a brush or a cloth to gently remove any dirt. This method is less likely to damage the eggshell and reduce the risk of contamination. In cases where washing is necessary, it is important to use warm water that is warmer than the egg itself, along with a mild detergent. This temperature differential helps to prevent the egg from absorbing water and potential contaminants through its porous shell. It is essential to avoid soaking the eggs, as this can lead to the absorption of contaminants, compromising the eggs' safety and quality.

Storing Eggs

Proper storage is key to maintaining the freshness of eggs. Eggs should be stored in a cool, dry place with an ideal temperature range between 45-55°F (7-13°C) and a humidity level of 70-80%. Such conditions help in slowing down the aging process and extending the eggs' shelf life. Refrigeration is highly recommended as it significantly extends the freshness of the eggs, keeping them viable for several weeks.

When storing eggs, it is beneficial to place them with the pointed end down. This orientation helps in maintaining the central position of the yolk and prevents the air cell from moving, which can affect the egg's quality over time. Ensuring that eggs are stored in a stable and optimal environment reduces the risk of spoilage and maintains their nutritional value.

TROUBLESHOOTING EGG PRODUCTION ISSUES

When egg production declines, promptly identifying and addressing the underlying issues is crucial for maintaining a productive flock. Several common problems can contribute to reduced egg production, each requiring specific attention and intervention.

Poor Nutrition: One of the most critical factors in egg production is the nutritional quality of the hens' diet. Hens require a balanced diet rich in essential nutrients to produce eggs consistently. Deficiencies in key nutrients such as calcium, phosphorus, and protein can significantly impact egg production. Calcium is particularly important for the formation of strong eggshells, while protein is vital for overall health and egg development. Ensure that the feed provided is specifically formulated for laying hens and meets all their dietary needs. Supplementing the diet with oyster shells or other calcium sources can help address calcium deficiencies. Regularly reviewing and adjusting the feed composition based on the hens' needs can prevent nutritional shortfalls that may lead to reduced egg production.

Inadequate Lighting: Lighting plays a significant role in regulating the laying cycles of hens. Insufficient light can disrupt their natural laying patterns, leading to a decline in egg production. Hens typically require 14-16 hours of light each day to maintain optimal egg production levels. Inadequate lighting, especially during shorter winter days, can be a common issue. Installing artificial lighting in the coop can help ensure that hens receive the necessary amount of light daily. Timers can be used to automate the lighting schedule, providing consistent light exposure and minimizing disruptions to the hens' laying cycles.

Health Problems: Regular health monitoring is essential to identify and address diseases, parasites, and other health issues that can affect egg production. Common ailments such as infectious bronchitis, egg drop syndrome, and various parasitic infections can lead to a decline in egg production. Early detection and treatment are crucial in managing these health problems. Observing the hens for any signs of illness, such as changes in behavior, appetite, or physical appearance, can help in early diagnosis. Consulting a veterinarian for a thorough examination and appropriate treatment is recommended to maintain the flock's health and productivity.

Stress Factors: Stress is a significant factor that can adversely affect egg production. Hens are sensitive to changes in their environment, and stress can stem from various sources such as predators, loud noises, or alterations in their living conditions. To minimize stress, it is important to provide a calm and stable environment for the hens. Ensure that their living quarters are secure from predators and free from excessive noise. Gradual transitions when introducing changes to their environment can also help reduce stress levels.

Aging Hens: It is important to recognize that egg production naturally declines as hens age. Older hens lay fewer eggs compared to younger ones. To maintain high production levels, it may be necessary to replace older hens with younger ones periodically. Monitoring the age and laying patterns of the hens can help in making timely decisions about flock management and replacement.

By addressing these common issues—ensuring proper nutrition, adequate lighting, health monitoring, stress management, and considering the age of the hens—egg production can be optimized and maintained at a high level. Regular evaluation and proactive management are key to sustaining a productive and healthy flock.

CHAPTER EIGHT

SUSTAINABILITY AND ADVANCED TOPICS

COMPOSTING AND USING CHICKEN MANURE

Composting chicken manure is a highly effective method for converting this potent waste product into valuable fertilizer that enhances soil health and promotes robust plant growth. Rich in nitrogen, phosphorus, and potassium—essential nutrients for plants—chicken manure requires composting to mitigate its potency and maximize its benefits.

Why Compost Chicken Manure?

Chicken manure, while nutrient-rich, is too strong to be applied directly to plants due to its high ammonia content, which can burn roots and foliage.

Composting addresses this issue by breaking down the manure through microbial action, thus reducing its ammonia levels and making nutrients more readily available to plants. This transformation from raw waste to stabilized compost not only makes it safer for plants but also optimizes its nutritional value for gardening purposes.

How to Compost Chicken Manure

The process of composting chicken manure involves several key steps:

1. Collecting Manure: Begin by regularly cleaning the chicken coop to gather fresh manure. Proper handling of manure is essential to prevent the

spread of pathogens and ensure optimal composting conditions.

2.   Mixing with Carbon-Rich Material: Combine the collected manure with carbon sources such as straw, leaves, or sawdust. This mixture balances the compost by providing the necessary carbon-to-nitrogen ratio, which helps prevent odors and supports the microbial activity essential for decomposition.

3.   Turning and Aerating: Regularly turn the compost pile to aerate it. Aerobic decomposition is crucial as it accelerates the breakdown of organic matter and prevents the pile from becoming anaerobic, which can lead to foul odors and inefficient composting.

4.   Curing: Allow the compost to cure for several weeks to months. During this curing period, microbial activity continues to break down organic materials, stabilizing the nutrients and ensuring the compost is mature and ready for use in the garden.

Benefits of Composting Chicken Manure

Composting chicken manure offers numerous benefits:

1.   Nutrient-Rich Soil: The compost enriches soil fertility by releasing nutrients such as nitrogen, phosphorus, and potassium gradually, providing a balanced diet for plants throughout their growth cycle.

2. Waste Reduction: It transforms poultry waste from a potential environmental pollutant into a valuable resource, minimizing the need for disposal and reducing the environmental footprint of poultry farming.

3. Environmental Sustainability: By substituting synthetic fertilizers with nutrient-rich compost, gardeners decrease reliance on chemicals that can harm soil structure and microbial diversity over time.

INTEGRATING CHICKENS WITH OTHER BACKYARD LIVESTOCK

Integrating chickens with other types of livestock, such as goats or rabbits, can greatly benefit both the animals and your homestead. This synergy offers various advantages ranging from enhanced dietary balance and pest control to efficient manure management. However, successful integration requires careful consideration of space, compatibility, and health management.

One of the primary benefits of integrating chickens with other livestock is their complementary diets. Chickens are efficient foragers, adept at picking insects and small vegetation, which helps control pests in the environment. This complements the feeding habits of larger animals like goats, who graze on grass and leaves. By utilizing different parts of the landscape and diverse food sources, these animals reduce competition for food and maximize the use of available resources.

Pest control is another significant advantage of integration. Chickens naturally consume insects, larvae, and even small rodents, contributing to pest management around the homestead. Their scratching behavior also disrupts pest habitats in the soil, further reducing populations. Larger animals such as goats or rabbits can deter predators through their size and presence, adding an extra layer of security for the chickens and other smaller livestock.

Effective manure management is crucial for maintaining soil fertility and health on a homestead. Integrating different types of livestock allows for the collection and composting of varied manures. Chickens produce nitrogen-rich droppings that are potent for accelerating decomposition in compost piles. When combined with the slower-degrading manure of goats or rabbits, the resulting compost becomes well-balanced and beneficial for enriching garden beds and crop fields.

However, integrating different livestock species requires careful consideration of several factors. Adequate space allocation is paramount to prevent overcrowding and reduce stress among animals. Each species needs sufficient room for grazing, foraging, and shelter, which should be tailored to their specific behavioral and physical requirements. Compatibility among animals is another crucial consideration. While chickens generally coexist well with goats or rabbits, individual personalities and territorial behaviors can vary. It's advisable to introduce animals gradually and monitor their interactions closely before fully integrating them into shared spaces. This approach minimizes the risk of aggression or stress-related issues.

Furthermore, managing the health of integrated livestock requires understanding their distinct needs. Chickens, goats, and rabbits may require different vaccinations, parasite control methods, and dietary supplements. Consulting with a veterinarian experienced in small livestock can provide guidance on preventive care and treatment protocols tailored to each species.

BREEDING CHICKENS

Breeding chickens is a deliberate process aimed at enhancing specific traits within a flock, such as egg production, meat quality, or particular physical characteristics. Prior to embarking on a breeding program, thorough research into breed standards and genetics is essential. This knowledge forms the foundation for achieving desired outcomes effectively.

Understanding breed standards is pivotal as it delineates the ideal characteristics for each breed. Traits such as plumage color, body size, egg color, and temperament vary widely among chicken breeds. By studying these standards, breeders gain insight into which traits to prioritize and how to select breeding stock accordingly.

The selection of breeding stock is a critical step that influences the success of breeding endeavors. Healthy, robust chickens that conform closely to breed standards are preferred choices. Vigorous birds are indicative of good genetic health and are more likely to produce offspring with desirable traits. Avoiding inbreeding is equally important to maintain genetic diversity within the flock, which helps in preventing genetic weaknesses and promoting overall flock resilience.

Detailed record-keeping is fundamental throughout the breeding process. Records should encompass information on breeding pairs, hatch rates, chick health, and any notable observations. These records serve as a guide for assessing progress, identifying successful breeding combinations, and making informed decisions for future breeding cycles.

Proper incubation and brooding techniques are indispensable for the health and survival of chicks. Incubation involves carefully regulating temperature, humidity, and ventilation to ensure optimal conditions for embryo development. Monitoring these parameters closely helps prevent developmental issues and ensures a higher hatch rate. Brooding, which follows incubation, involves providing warmth, shelter, and appropriate nutrition to newly hatched chicks. Adequate space, access to clean water, and balanced nutrition are crucial during this phase to support healthy growth and development.

Genetics play a pivotal role in breeding chickens, influencing traits that are passed down from parent birds to their offspring. Understanding basic genetic principles such as dominant and recessive traits, as well as genetic inheritance patterns, allows breeders to predict outcomes more accurately. This knowledge facilitates strategic breeding decisions aimed at consolidating desirable traits over successive generations.

Beyond genetics, factors such as environmental conditions, nutrition, and healthcare also impact the overall health and productivity of the flock. Providing a clean and suitable living environment, balanced nutrition tailored to the birds' developmental stages, and implementing preventive healthcare measures are integral to fostering optimal growth and performance.

EXPANDING YOUR FLOCK AND ADVANCED CARE TECHNIQUES

Expanding your poultry flock is an exciting endeavor that requires meticulous planning and consideration of various factors to ensure the well-being and productivity of your birds. Before acquiring additional chickens, it's crucial to assess your available space, resources, and goals. Determining the maximum number of chickens your setup can comfortably accommodate is essential for maintaining optimal living conditions and avoiding overcrowding, which can lead to stress and health issues.

When preparing to expand, adequate housing is paramount. Ensure that your coop and run provide enough space per bird to allow for natural behaviors such as roosting, nesting, and foraging. Proper ventilation, insulation against extreme weather, and predator-proofing are also critical aspects to consider in the design and maintenance of your chicken housing.

Feeding and nutrition play a vital role in the health and productivity of your flock. As you expand, review your feeding regimen to ensure all chickens receive a balanced diet suitable for their age and purpose, whether it's egg production or meat development. Specialized diets may be necessary, depending on the stage of growth or specific goals you have for your chickens.

Introducing new birds to an existing flock requires careful management of flock dynamics. Chickens establish a pecking order, and introducing newcomers can disrupt this hierarchy, leading to aggression. To minimize stress and aggression, introduce new chickens gradually, ideally in a separate but adjacent space to allow for acclimatization while still within sight of the existing flock.

Advanced care techniques are essential for maintaining the health and disease resistance of your chickens. Implementing a regular health check-up schedule allows you to monitor individual bird health and detect early signs of illness. Vaccination against common poultry diseases, according to recommended schedules, provides proactive protection and reduces the risk of disease outbreaks within your flock.

Biosecurity measures are critical to prevent the introduction and spread of diseases. Establish strict protocols for sanitation, including disinfecting equipment and limiting visitor access to your flock area. Quarantine new birds before introducing them to your existing flock to ensure they are healthy and disease-free.

Understanding common poultry diseases and their symptoms enables prompt intervention and treatment when necessary. Familiarize yourself with disease symptoms such as respiratory distress, diarrhea, or abnormal behavior to respond swiftly and effectively.

Continuously educate yourself on advancements in poultry care and management practices. Stay updated on new research, innovations in housing and nutrition, and evolving disease management strategies. Networking with other poultry enthusiasts and professionals can provide valuable insights and support as you expand and enhance your flock.

By prioritizing careful planning, proactive health management, and ongoing education, you can successfully expand your poultry flock while ensuring the well-being and productivity of your chickens for years to come.

THE END